NOV    2006

# THE CREATION OF
# SPIDER-MAN ®

## PAUL KUPPERBERG

The Rosen Publishing Group, Inc.,
New York

*To Stan and Steve and the rest of the Mighty Marvel Bullpen.*
*Excelsior, true believers!*

Published in 2007 by The Rosen Publishing Group, Inc.
29 East 21st Street, New York, NY 10010

Thanks to Marvel Entertainment, Inc.: Avi Arad, James Hinton, Mary Law, Bruno Maglione, Tim Rothwell, Mickey Stern, Alberta Stewart, and Carl Suecoff

### Library of Congress Cataloging-in-Publication Data

Kupperberg, Paul.
The creation of spider-man/Paul Kupperberg.—1st ed.
    p. cm.—(Action Heroes)
Includes bibliographical references and index.
ISBN 1-4042-0763-5 (library binding)
1. Spider-Man (Comic strip) 2. Spider-Man (Fictitious character) I. Title. II. Series.
PN6728.S6K87 2006
741.5'973—dc22

2005033258

*Manufactured in the United States of America*

**On the cover:** Spider-Man swings into action.

# CONTENTS

INTRODUCTION 5

1 THE SECRET ORIGINS OF STAN AND STEVE 8

2 THE TIMELY BIRTH OF MARVEL COMICS 14

3 DOES WHATEVER A SPIDER CAN 22

4 WITH GREAT POWER COMES GREAT RESPONSIBILITY 29

5 MULTIMEDIA HERO 34

TIMELINE: STAN LEE AND STEVE DITKO 41

SPIDER-MAN HIGHLIGHTS 42

GLOSSARY 43

FOR MORE INFORMATION 44

FOR FURTHER READING 45

BIBLIOGRAPHY 46

INDEX 47

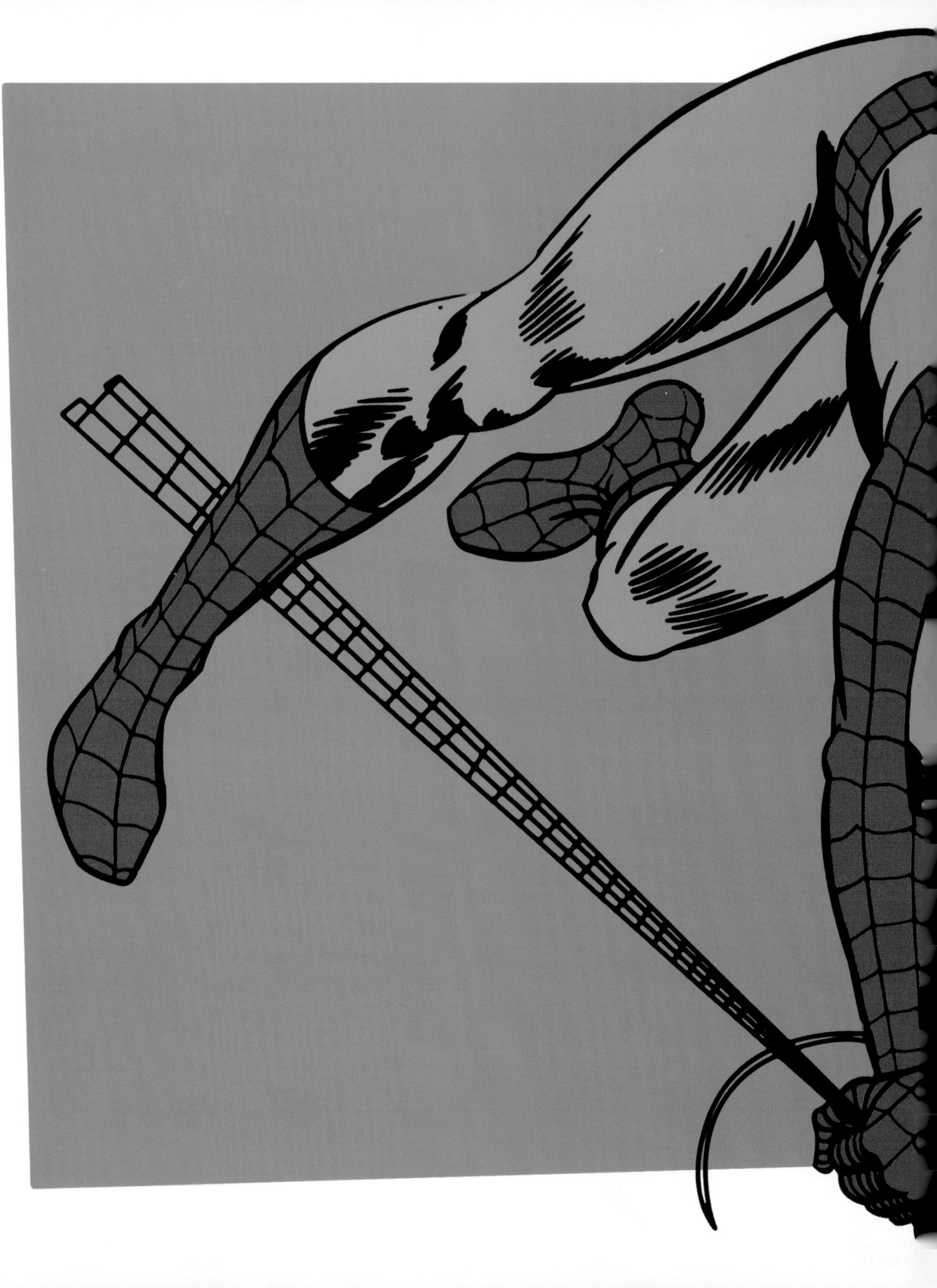

There were two things that a reader picking up an issue of *Amazing Fantasy* #15 (August 1962) did not know. The first was that this was the last issue of the magazine's short run. The other was that it would turn out to be one of the most significant comic books of its time. It featured the debut of Spider-Man. At first glance, however, there was not much to separate Spider-Man from the rest of the Super Heroes then appearing in the comic books on America's newsstands.

The Super Hero genre had been a comic book mainstay beginning with the introduction of Superman in *Action Comics* #1 (June 1938). Timely Comics was particularly good at taking advantage of comic trends. The company published endless variations in whatever genre was selling at a particular time. Following this method, Timely writers created such Super Hero powerhouses as Captain America, the Human

Torch, and the Sub-Mariner. But eventually, readers' interest shifted to other genres. As a result, Super Hero comics barely outlived War World II (1939–1945).

At the beginning of the 1960s, however, DC Comics was having some success with updated series that revived their stable of 1940s Super Heroes. DC scored a big hit with the Justice League of America, which first appeared in *The Brave and the Bold* #28 (June 1960). Before long, Timely Comics responded with a Super Hero revival of its own. The publisher, which by 1960 had changed its name to Atlas, began releasing *The Fantastic Four* (November 1961). But the Fantastic Four, and the Atlas heroes who followed them, were unlike any that had come before.

For example, Spider-Man's superpowers were nothing too original. The hero had superstrength, the ability to scale walls and walk across ceilings, and a sixth sense (his so-called spider-sense) that warned him of impending danger. What was original, however, was the fact that outside of his Super Hero identity, he was nerdy high school student Peter Parker. The bite of a spider in a laboratory accident had turned the scrawny loser into the wall-crawling, friendly neighborhood Spider-Man.

But Parker remained the bullied and ignored nerd whenever he was out of costume. Even as Spider-Man, Parker had his troubles. The newspaper publisher J. Jonah Jameson took to disliking the new Super Hero and used the resources of the *Daily Bugle* to make Spider-Man out to be a villain.

Going against the standard formula, the Spider-Man story mixed the familiar Super Hero concept with heavy doses of soap opera and elements of melodrama. Spider-Man's co-creators, writer Stan Lee and artist Steve Ditko, had created something new in the world of comic books: the flawed hero with everyday problems. This super man had a real life.

It would take a few years, but that idea would spawn a comics revolution.

# 1 THE SECRET ORIGINS OF STAN AND STEVE

By the late 1960s, the names of the Marvel artists and writers were well known to their many fans. The Marvel Comics Bullpen, as the team came to be known, included Stan Lee, Steve Ditko, Jack Kirby, and others. The men in this creative clique were cultural pop stars, making cameo appearances in the pages of their own comics and in the mass media.

Lee and his artist co-creators sparked a revolution. Comics were suddenly taken seriously, seen by many as modern mythological literature. Unlike before, comics were read by college students, analyzed by academics, and used as inspiration by fine artists and filmmakers alike. Stan Lee had always wanted to have an impact on American culture by one day writing the great American novel. But more than twenty years into a very different

Stan Lee poses with a friend in a Spider-Man costume at Universal City, California, in August 2002. The two were there to celebrate the Super Hero's fortieth birthday. Marvel's superheroes and villains are featured attractions at the Universal Studios resorts and theme parks. Among the most popular figures are Spider-Man, Hulk, and Captain America—all co-created by Stan Lee and the artists of Marvel Comics.

sort of writing career, he found himself being recognized as the guru behind the comics revolution of the 1960s.

## THE QUINTESSENTIAL HACK

Stan Lee was born Stanley Martin Lieber on December 28, 1922. He was the first child of Jack and Celia Lieber of New York City. His father worked in New York's garment district. However, after the stock market crash of 1929, Jack Lieber found it difficult to get steady work. Ultimately, he had to move his family to the Bronx, New York.

After graduating in 1939 from DeWitt Clinton High School, Stan found a job as a gofer. This means he was the person the editor

## EARLY INFLUENCES

Many of the talents and skills for which Stan Lee would one day become famous could be seen developing in young Stanley Lieber. His legendary imagination was fed by the constant reading he did to escape the sadness and poverty of his home life. Among his favorites were the adventures of Franklin W. Dixon's Hardy Boys and the works of H. G. Wells, Sir Arthur Conan Doyle, Mark Twain, Edgar Rice Burroughs, Edgar Allan Poe, Charles Dickens, and Shakespeare.

Stan also loved the great adventure films of his youth. He spent countless hours in the neighborhood movie theaters with such characters as King Kong, Sherlock Holmes, Gunga Din, and Frankenstein. By his early teen years, Lieber also had comic books to fuel his ideas. These books featured reprints of such newspaper comic strips as *Dick Tracy*, the *Katzenjammer Kids*, and *Tarzan*.

Stan dabbled in writing, too, entering newspaper essay contests. While still in high school, he wrote obituaries for a wire service. Other jobs helped him develop skills he would use later in his career to promote himself and Marvel Comics. These included selling newspaper subscriptions to his fellow students and working as an actor. For the second position, he worked with the Works Progress Administration's Federal Theater Project, a Depression-era government program that supplied jobs to the unemployed.

could send to "go fer" coffee or whatever else was needed. For his efforts, Stan made eight dollars a week. The company was Timely Comics, owned by Martin Goodman, Stan's cousin by marriage. The editor at Timely was the comics pioneer Joe Simon. Along with his partner, Jack Kirby, Simon co-created the popular *Captain America* strip.

Stan could not have picked two better tutors than Simon and Kirby to teach him the business of comic books. Simon was multitalented: he was a writer, artist, and crackerjack businessman. Kirby, for his part, was defining the visual vocabulary and power of early comic book storytelling.

Stan planned to one day write serious literature under his real name. So he used the pseudonym "Stan Lee" (his first name broken into two syllables) for his comic book work. Lee's first published story appeared in *Captain America* #3 (May 1941). His initial comic script was written for "Headline Hunter, Foreign Correspondent," which began in *Captain America* #5 (August 1941). It would be the first of thousands of scripts to come.

In late 1941, Simon and Kirby were lured away by a rival publisher. So Goodman chose the nineteen-year-old Lee to be Timely's editor. Except for the three years Lee would soon spend in military service, it was a job he would hold for decades.

Stan Lee established himself as the company's most prolific writer. In his autobiography, he called himself "the ultimate, quintessential hack." (A hack is someone without very high standards who will do any work, as long as it pays.) If he was a hack, at least he was a versatile one, penning stories in whatever genre was then

AND, A FEW MINUTES LATER, PETER PARKER FORGETS THE TAUNTS OF HIS CLASSMATES AS HE IS TRANSPORTED TO ANOTHER WORLD-- THE FASCINATING WORLD OF ATOMIC SCIENCE!

AND NOW FOR A DEMONSTRATION OF HOW WE CAN CONTROL RADIOACTIVE RAYS HERE IN THE LABORATORY...

BUT, AS THE EXPERIMENT BEGINS, NO ONE NOTICES A TINY SPIDER, DESCENDING FROM THE CEILING ON AN ALMOST INVISIBLE STRAND OF WEB...

A SPIDER WHOM FATE HAS GIVEN A STARRING, IF BRIEF, ROLE TO PLAY IN THE DRAMA WE CALL LIFE!

ACCIDENTALLY ABSORBING A FANTASTIC AMOUNT OF RADIOACTIVITY, THE DYING INSECT, IN SUDDEN SHOCK, BITES THE NEAREST LIVING THING, AT THE SPLIT SECOND BEFORE LIFE EBBS FROM ITS RADIOACTIVE BODY!

OW!

A-A SPIDER! IT BIT ME! BUT, WHY IS IT BURNING SO? WHY IS IT GLOWING THAT WAY??

MY HEAD-- IT FEELS STRANGE! I-I NEED SOME AIR!

LOOKS AS THOUGH OUR EX-PERIMENT UNNERVED YOUNG PARKER!

TOO BAD! HE MUST HAVE A WEAK STOMACH!

WHAT'S *HAPPENING* TO ME? I FEEL-- DIFFERENT! AS THOUGH MY ENTIRE BODY IS CHARGED WITH SOME SORT OF FANTASTIC ENERGY!

HONK! HONK!

WRAPPED IN HIS THOUGHTS, PETER DOESN'T HEAR THE AUTO WHICH NARROWLY MISSES HIM, UNTIL THE LAST INSTANT! AND THEN, UNNOTICED BY THE RIDERS, HE UNTHINKINGLY LEAPS TO SAFETY-- BUT WHAT A LEAP IT IS!

THAT WAS *ONE* EGGHEAD WHO WON'T DAYDREAM ANY MORE WHEN HE CROSSES A STREET!

YOU CAN SAY *THAT* AGAIN!

**Unlike most other comic book artists, Steve Ditko drew characters who looked like real people, not exaggerated muscle-men. His teenage Peter Parker is seen in this page from *Amazing Fantasy #15* (August 1962), the issue that introduced Spider-Man to the public. Parker's story attracted older readers who had outgrown simpler Super Hero comics.**

selling. But by 1960, Lee had lost interest in comics and longed to move on to other sorts of writing.

## STEVE DITKO, ARTIST OF DISTINCTION

Stan Lee is one of comics' most public men. His *Spider-Man* collaborator, Steve Ditko, is one of the most private. Ditko prefers to let his work speak for itself.

Steve Ditko was born in Johnstown, Pennsylvania, on November 2, 1927. As a youngster, he was a fan of comic books. He especially liked *Batman* and *The Spirit*, a Sunday newspaper comic supplement created by the legendary Will Eisner. Eisner was a comic author who pioneered the graphic novel in the 1970s and helped make comics a legitimate art form. Ditko learned to draw by copying the art in Eisner's comics, although his own style would veer off into a very different direction.

After graduating high school, Ditko moved to New York and studied at the Cartoonists and Illustrators School. One of his teachers and greatest influences there was Jerry Robinson. Robinson was a veteran artist whose body of work included the early *Batman* stories Ditko read and admired as a youngster.

By the mid-1950s, Ditko was freelancing for Stan Lee at Timely Comics, which was generally known as Atlas Comics during this period. At the same time, he was also doing work for Charlton Comics, a minor publisher based in Derby, Connecticut. Charlton produced a line of romance and other genre titles. Ditko's style was far removed from the stereotypical square-jawed comic hero. His people were real and vulnerable. His style was distinctive and moody, and his characters were overly yet effectively emotive. He was the perfect artist for stories that had a psychological aspect. Ditko was Lee's first choice for such stories. In fact, Lee had designed the horror comic anthology *Amazing Adult Fantasy* (December 1961) specifically to showcase Ditko's art.

*Amazing Adult Fantasy*, soon renamed simply *Amazing Fantasy*, featured all sorts of short, imaginative fantasy strips with surprise endings. Lee loved these stories, and he thought that Ditko illustrated them brilliantly. However, not enough readers bought *Amazing Fantasy*, so Lee decided to do one last issue and then let the book rest in peace.

That ending would prove the start of something readers would buy.

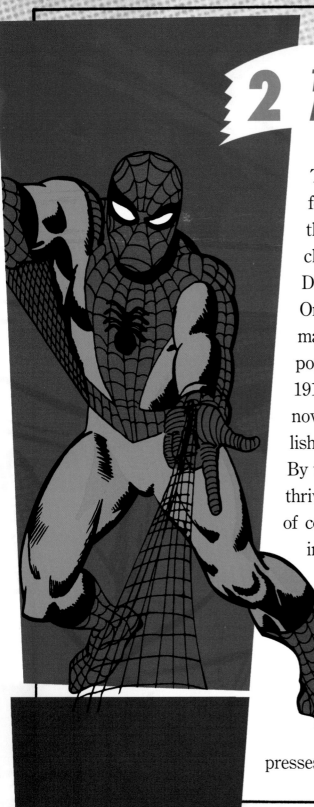

## 2 THE TIMELY BIRTH OF MARVEL COMICS

The comic strip had been a popular feature in newspapers since at least the 1890s. The form spawned such characters as Buster Brown, Popeye, Dick Tracy, Buck Rogers, and Little Orphan Annie. Inexpensive fiction magazines called pulps started gaining popularity around the same time. In 1912, Edgar Rice Burroughs's famous novel *Tarzan of the Apes* was published in the pulp *All-Story Magazine*. By the 1930s, 10¢ pulp magazines were thriving. They featured their own array of costumed superpower heroes, including the Shadow and G-8. In addition, there were scores of other titles in every genre from westerns to crime to romance and beyond.

The first comic books were conceived in 1933 as promotional giveaways and as a way to keep idle printing presses busy. Companies like Proctor &

Gamble and Kinney Shoes thought they could increase their visibility through promotional comic books. When customers purchased their products, they also received free magazines that contained reprints of newspaper comic strips. The companies hoped children would increase demand for the products because they wanted the comics. These early comic magazines—with titles like *Funnies on Parade* and *A Century of Comics*—were the first comic books. Soon enough, enterprising publishers put a 10¢ price tag on these new comic books and offered them for sale on newsstands. They proved to be popular.

During the 1930s, pulp magazines were among the best-sellers at newsstands like the one shown here. By the end of the decade, the new comic book format was replacing pulps in popularity.

The magazines were soon followed by titles that printed new material, including *New Fun* (February 1935) and *New Comics* (December 1935). In 1937, DC Comics' *Detective Comics* #1 (March) was the first comic featuring stories based on a single theme. But it

No. 1      JUNE, 1938

# ACTION COMICS

10¢

The comic book craze began with *Action Comics* #1 (June 1938). This title introduced Superman, the medium's first costumed Super Hero. Co-created by writer Jerry Siegel and artist Joe Shuster, Superman became multimillion-dollar property. The character starred in films and newspaper comic strips and on radio programs. His image also appeared on countless licensed products, such as toys and lunch boxes.

took the introduction of Superman for comics to have their first superstar. With his arrival, in 1938, the burgeoning industry got the boost that would turn comics into a mass medium read by kids across America.

## THE GOLDEN AGE OF COMICS

Working out of New York City, Martin Goodman began publishing magazines and pulps in the 1930s. Among his titles were *Star Detective*, *Marvel Science Stories*, and *Marvel Tales*. Then, in 1939, he decided to get into the new comic book business.

Goodman's initial comic publication was *Marvel Comics* #1 (October 1939), featuring the Human Torch and the Sub-Mariner. Goodman published the issue under the name Timely Comics, a division of his company that he created specifically for releasing new comic titles. The patriotic hero Captain America joined the Timely Comics ranks in March 1941, and his magazine quickly became the company's best-selling title.

As with most of the publishers that flourished in comics' early years, Timely found that the Super Hero was its mainstay. *Superman* and *Captain Marvel* eventually sold in excess of one million copies per issue. *Captain America* was exceptional, selling nearly one million copies with its very first issue.

But soon after World War II, circulation began to fall. Publishers started looking for something other than superheroes to sell their books. By 1947, funny animals and westerns were replacing the costumed crime fighters on the comics pages.

## TIGHTENING THE BELT

By the mid-1950s, comic sales were declining, due in part to the growing popularity of television. In addition, various groups had begun to criticize comic books as being dangerous to children. Dr. Frederic Wertham led the charge against comics. He was a respected psychiatrist who had written a popular book, *Seduction of the Innocent* (1954), which blamed comic books for spurring violent behavior in otherwise normal young people.

As an expert on juvenile behavior, Wertham advised the U.S. Senate's Subcommittee on Juvenile Delinquency. The report published by this committee in 1955 concluded that comic books offered very little of value. As a result, Americans began to turn away.

In 1957, a change in distributors forced Martin Goodman's company, by then known as Atlas, to limit his line to eight published titles a month. The reduced Atlas line limped along for several years, releasing science fiction and monster stories. These were competently written and well drawn by talents like Kirby, Ditko, Joe Maneely, and Don Heck. However, they were less than satisfying, creatively.

Lee wrote in his 2002 autobiography, *Excelsior!*, "By the early 1960s, my urge to quit the comic book field had become stronger than ever . . . There was nothing new coming along to pique the readers' interest."

But just as Lee was on the verge of quitting, Goodman asked him to create a team of Super Heroes similar to DC's Justice League of America. According to Lee, his wife, Joanie, encouraged him to use this opportunity to create brand-new heroes and write them in a different style, the style he had always wanted to use. This style, Lee thought, might attract older readers as well as the young ones. "Remember," Joanie said, "you've got nothing to lose by doing the book your way. The worst that can happen is that Martin will get mad and fire you; but you want to quit anyway, so what's the risk?"

## THE MIGHTY MARVEL AGE

The result was the creation of the Fantastic Four. This was a team of four friends who had been transformed into Super Heroes when they encountered cosmic rays on a space mission. By 1962, it was clear that Lee's experiment was paying off. The fan reaction to the Fantastic Four was overwhelmingly positive, stronger by far than for any other title then in Lee's lineup.

## COMIC BOOKS AND THE RED MENACE

Marvel's new heroes were clearly rooted in the cold war paranoia of their day. The cold war was a period during which the Soviet Union and the United States fought for global supremacy. Both nations built up their nuclear arsenals and threatened each other with annihilation. With this as the historical backdrop, Marvel's story arcs focused on the threat of Soviet Communism and Americans' fear of nuclear power and the atomic bomb.

- The Fantastic Four took their life-altering space voyage in an attempt to beat the Communists into space orbit.

- The Hulk was born out of the fire of a gamma-ray bomb that had been detonated by a Communist spy in an effort to kill its creator.

- Thanks to his laboratory discoveries, biochemist Dr. Henry Pym became Ant-Man. As Ant-Man, Pym shrank down to insect size and used his power to fight Communist agents. He was motivated by the idea of being able to fit an entire army into a single plane, thinking that this would facilitate American troop movements.

- Iron Man created his super armor to save himself from a life-threatening wound suffered when Communist forces in Vietnam captured him.

- Thor, a character rooted in classic Norse mythology, fought alien invaders. But the aliens' motive of world domination was just a thinly veiled reference to the perceived goal of the Communists in the Soviet Union.

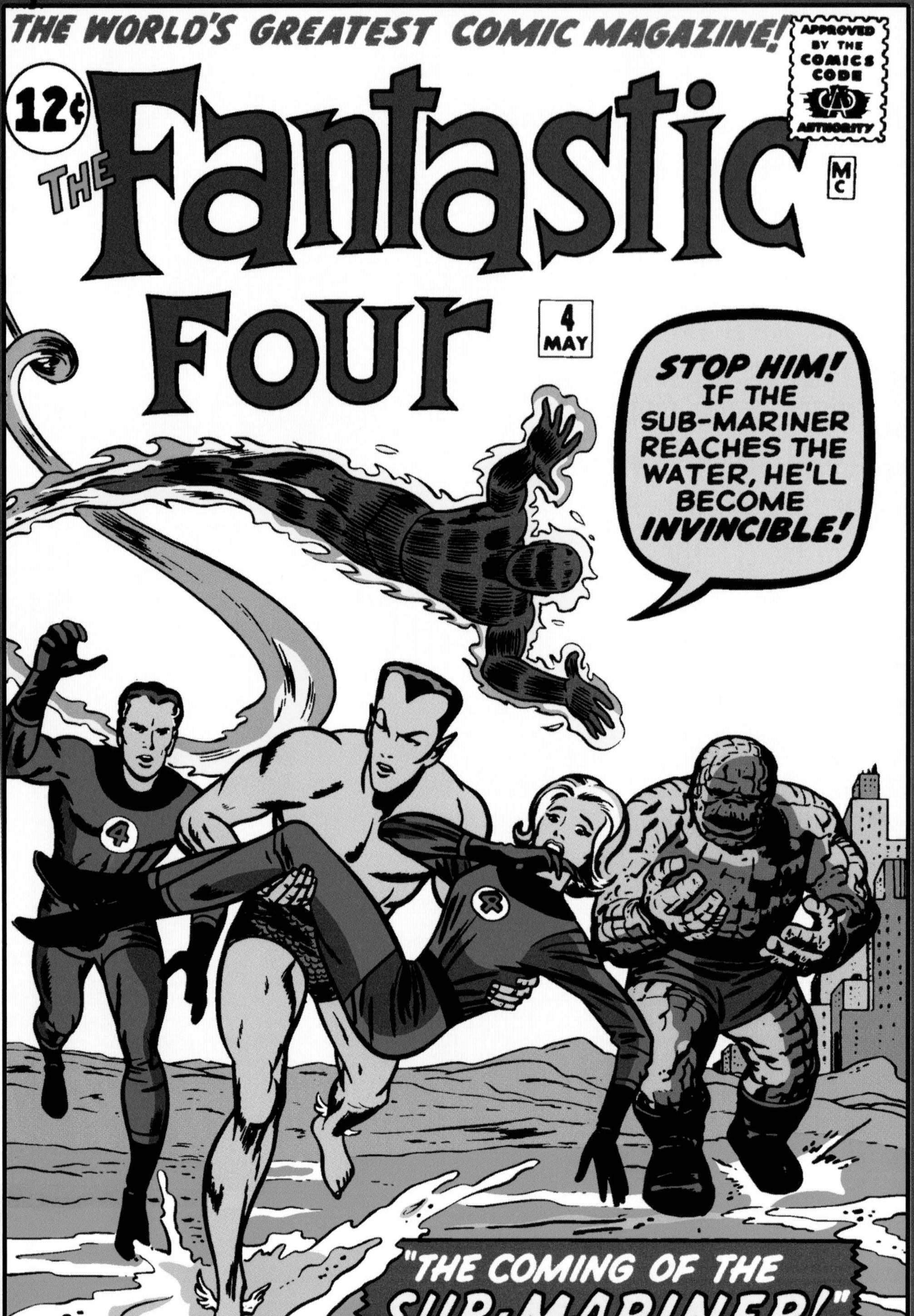
THE WORLD'S GREATEST COMIC MAGAZINE!
APPROVED BY THE COMICS CODE AUTHORITY
12¢
THE Fantastic FOUR
MC
4 MAY
STOP HIM! IF THE SUB-MARINER REACHES THE WATER, HE'LL BECOME INVINCIBLE!
"THE COMING OF THE SUB-MARINER!"

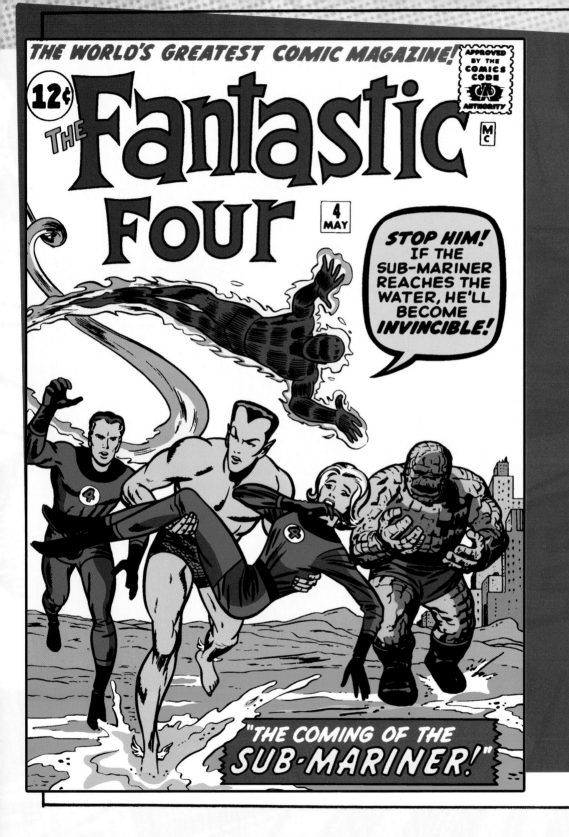

Encouraged by this success, Goodman allowed Lee to continue adding Super Heroes to the line. After May 1963, the line carried the "Marvel Comics" imprint on its covers. The Fantastic Four were followed by Ant-Man, who first appeared in *Tales to Astonish* #27 (January 1962); the Incredible Hulk, first appearing in *The Incredible Hulk* #1 (May 1962); Thor, first appearing in *Journey into Mystery* #83 (August 1962); Iron Man, debuting in *Tales of Suspense* #39 (March 1963); and Doctor Strange, introduced in *Strange Tales* #110 (July 1963).

Stan Lee's new approach to the old idea of the Super Hero slowly took shape. His stories were not just about heroes battling villains. Nor were they just gimmicky tales based on some obscure scientific fact. Instead, they were about the people underneath the costumes and the way their newfound superpowers changed their lives. His series took the Super Heroes and made them very much human.

Then along came a radioactive spider.

**In November 1961, struggling Atlas Comics published *The Fantastic Four* #1. Compared to other Super Hero comics of the time, *The Fantastic Four* was more realistic and complex. At left is issue #4 of *The Fantastic Four* (May 1963), which marked the return of the Sub-Mariner. He had been one of the most popular Atlas Comics characters in the 1940s.**

# 3 DOES WHATEVER A SPIDER CAN

Lee was tired of the old way of doing comic book superheroes. He wanted to create characters who would be more realistic and challenging to write. For several months, he had been thinking about just such a realistic hero. This one would possess some superstrength, but his main power would be the ability to stick to walls and ceilings. The most interesting part of this new hero, whom he wanted to call Spider-Man, would be his personal life. He would be a teenager rather than an adult. He would be a bit of a nerd, with all the problems of a typical teen. Lee took this radical new idea to his boss, Martin Goodman.

## CREATIVE DIFFERENCES

Goodman was less than enthusiastic. At first, Goodman gave Stan Lee every reason why

Spider-Man would never work. He told Lee that teens could be sidekicks to adult Super Heroes but not Super Heroes themselves. He pointed out that heroes did not have personal problems because these only slowed down the fast-paced action of Super Hero stories. Lee's nerdy, allergic Spider-Man sounded more comedic than heroic. And anyway, nobody wanted to read about a character named Spider-Man; people hated spiders!

But Lee couldn't get Spider-Man out of his mind. Since Goodman would not approve a new magazine for this hero, Lee decided instead to feature him in the final issue of *Amazing Fantasy*. Remembering what his wife had said, Lee reasoned that the publisher would not care too much about what went into the last issue of a canceled title.

One of Lee's frequent collaborators, Jack Kirby, was originally given the story to draw. However, Kirby's muscular, heroic style was wrong for the nerdy, frail main character, Peter Parker. In short order, Jack Kirby was out, and Steve Ditko was brought in to replace him.

## STEVE DITKO, CO-CREATOR

In an essay that appeared in an issue of *Robin Snyder's History of Comics*, Steve Ditko wrote that the five Kirby-penciled Spider-Man pages he received from Lee "showed a teenager living with his kindly old aunt and hard, gruff, retired police captain uncle . . . who was hostile toward the boy . . . Next door or somewhere in the neighborhood there was a whiskered scientist-type involved in some kind of experiment or project. The end of the five pages depicted the kid going toward the scientist's darkened house."

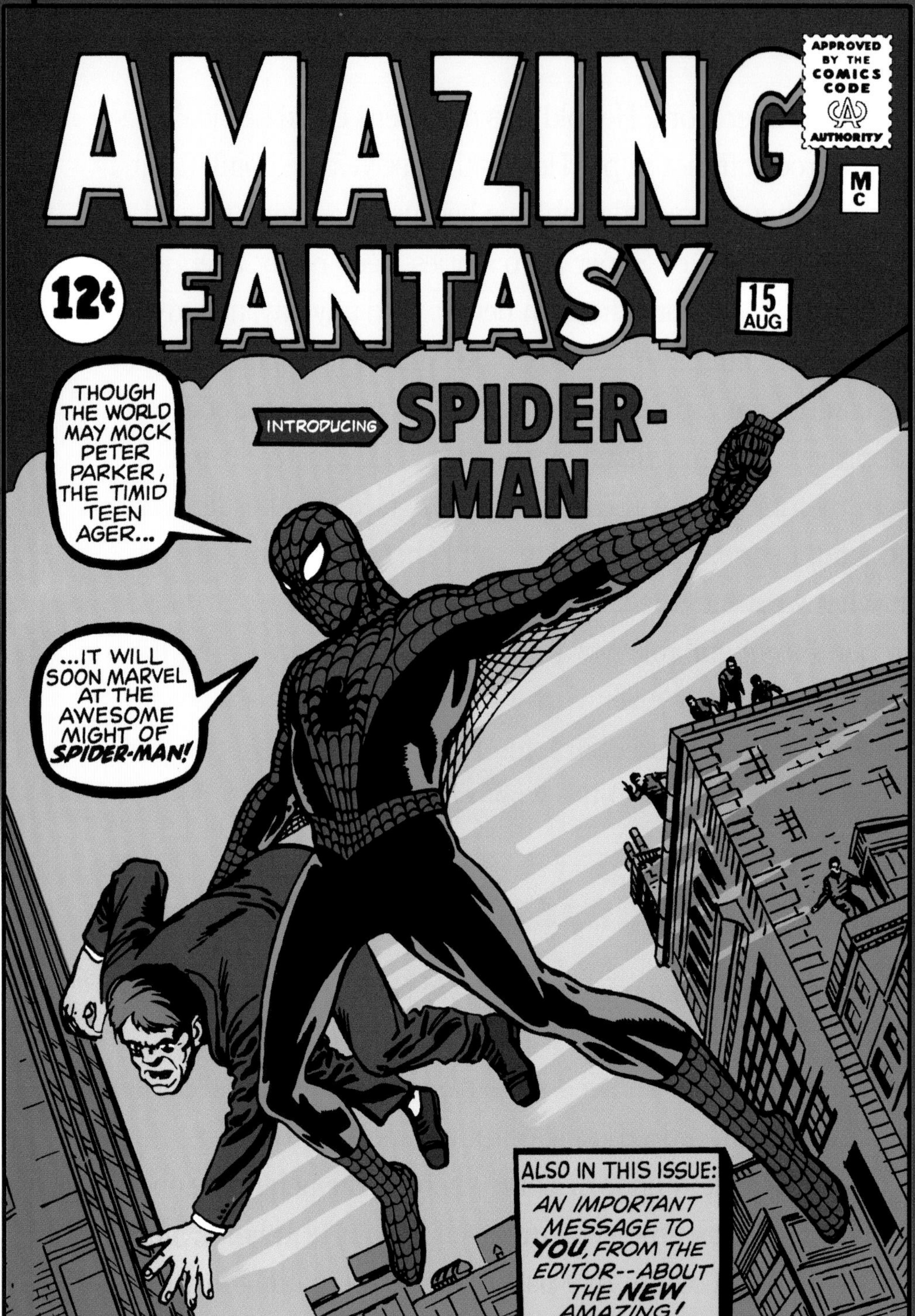

AMAZING
FANTASY
12¢
15 AUG
APPROVED BY THE COMICS CODE AUTHORITY
MC
THOUGH THE WORLD MAY MOCK PETER PARKER, THE TIMID TEEN AGER...
INTRODUCING SPIDER-MAN
...IT WILL SOON MARVEL AT THE AWESOME MIGHT OF SPIDER-MAN!
ALSO IN THIS ISSUE:
AN IMPORTANT MESSAGE TO YOU, FROM THE EDITOR--ABOUT THE NEW AMAZING!

Ditko saw an opportunity to do a more complex character than the one envisioned by Lee and Kirby. So, working from an outline and Kirby's original pages, he produced the image of the character that would drive its story for decades. Our hero, Peter Parker, ended up with bottle-thick glasses, slumped shoulders, and a homemade costume. The Spider-Man millions of readers came to know and love got his youth and voice from Stan Lee. The essence of his human frailty, however, came from the inspired artistry of Steve Ditko.

As an artist, Ditko knew the most important elements of the comic book medium. In a 1990 essay, Ditko wrote, "One of the first things I did was to work up a costume. A vital, visual part of the character. I had to know how he looked, to fit in with the powers he had, or could have, the possible gimmicks and how they might be used and shown, before I did any breakdowns . . . I wasn't sure Stan would like the idea of covering the character's face, but I did it because it hid an obvious boyish face."

Lee was more than pleased with Ditko's contributions to Spider-Man. He found Ditko's subtle yet highly stylized way of drawing to be perfect for the way he envisioned Spider-Man.

**By the early 1960s, Atlas Comics—soon to be called Marvel Comics—was poised to spark a comic book revolution. The key moment came with the creation of Spider-Man, who was introduced in *Amazing Fantasy* #15 (August 1962). By the end of the decade, Spider-Man had grown into an icon, rivaling Superman in popularity. A mint copy of the comic book with Spider-Man's first appearance *(cover shown at left)* sold at auction for $44,275 in 2002.**

MARVEL'S MERRY MADMEN ARE EXCEPTIONALLY PROUD OF STEVE DITKO'S SUPERB PORTRAYAL OF SPIDER-MAN IN ACTION, DRAWN ESPECIALLY TO DEMONSTRATE HIS AGILITY AND HIS ALMOST UNBELIEVABLE POWERS OF COORDINATION! AS A FAST-MOVING, QUICK-THINKING ACROBATIC STUNT-MAN, THE OL' WEB-SPINNER IS UNDENIABLY WITHOUT PEER... JUST AS SENSATIONAL STEVE IS TOPS IN PRESENTING SPIDEY'S UNIQUE BRAND OF LIGHTNING-SWIFT ACTION!

START HERE FOR SPIDEY'S LIVING ACTION DEMONSTRATION

**Steve Ditko's unique drawing style made him one of comics' most admired artists. His characters are often shown bending and twisting in ways that seem impossible yet look convincing. Ditko's Spider-Man has a power and grace that subsequent artists have tried to duplicate. For Spider-Man live-action movies, the special effects departments tried, too, to re-create Ditko's dynamic style.**

## THE MARVEL METHOD

In order to maximize his writing output, Stan Lee had veered from the usual method of comic book writing. Traditionally, the format of a comic book script was very similar to a movie screenplay. It broke down the action page by page and panel by panel. The art description was provided for each panel, along with the dialogue and sound effects.

This method, however, was time consuming. In order to save time, Lee provided his artists with a brief plot outline. To save even more time, he often passed this information along verbally. The artist would then pencil the story based on this outline, adding his own ideas to the broad concept Lee gave him. When the artist was finished, Lee would write the dialogue based on the artist's drawings and notes.

Lee's method, which came to be known as the Marvel Method, gave the artist far greater input into the creation of the story than the old method. The Marvel Method allowed the artists to control the pacing of the story and to add anything from subtle character bits to major story points.

## A QUESTION OF CREDIT

Jack Kirby's memories of the genesis of Spider-Man differ from Stan Lee's. In an interview from July 1982, Kirby remembered that the idea was already in place when he talked to Lee. According to Kirby, he and Joe Simon already had a script they called "The Silver Spider," which had a main character he believed could become a hero called Spider-Man.

Joe Simon had yet another take on the origin of Spider-Man. According to Simon in *The Comic Book Makers*, the Simon and Kirby creation the Fly (written for Archie Comics) began as a character they had called first Spiderman and then the Silver Spider. As Simon told the story, "Jack brought in the Spiderman logo I had loaned to him before we changed the name . . . Kirby laid out the story to Lee about the kid who finds a ring in a spider web, gets his powers from the ring and goes forth to fight crime armed with The Silver Spider's old web-spinning pistol."

After Lee replaced Kirby with Ditko, Simon said, "Ditko ignored Kirby's pages, tossed the character's magic ring, web-pistol, and goggles into a handy wastebasket, and completely redesigned Spider-Man's costume and equipment. In this life, he became high school student Peter Parker who gets his spider powers after being bitten by a radioactive spider."

When Spider-Man debuted in *Amazing Fantasy* #15, the only thing left of Jack Kirby's contribution was the character's name, with the addition of a hyphen. Kirby is also credited with penciling the cover, which Ditko inked.

Marvel's artists approached this freedom in different ways. Jack Kirby used the opportunity to add his unique brand of high-energy, dynamic story concepts. Steve Ditko's contributions, on the other hand, were far subtler. He tended to explore the deeper psychological aspects of his characters. Working from Stan Lee's plots, Ditko was able to create a character grounded in reality and familiar to his teenage readers. His Spider-Man story emerged as an honest portrayal of teenage life. At the same time, the real-life story was mixed in with fast-paced superhero action and a gallery of interesting and sometimes bizarre super-villain opponents.

"In those days it took about two or three months to get the final sales figures of any publication," Lee remembered in *Excelsior!* "When those sales reports finally came in, they showed that the Spider-Man issue [of *Amazing Fantasy*] had been a smash success, perhaps the best-selling comic book of the whole decade!"

Seven months later, the web-crawler became a headliner with the publication of *The Amazing Spider-Man* #1 (March 1963). Spider-Man emerged as the prototypical Marvel Comics character: the hero whose great powers are also a burden that he is forced to bear. By 1965, Stan Lee and Spider-Man were rapidly on their way to becoming American icons.

# 4 WITH GREAT POWER COMES GREAT RESPONSIBILITY

By the late 1950s, comics were no longer a very popular medium in American society. "To the public at large," Lee wrote in *Excelsior!*, "comics were at the very bottom of the cultural totem pole. Most of the adult world didn't buy them, care about them, or want their children to 'waste their time reading them.'"

## FROM JUNK TO POP ART

The emergence and subsequent popularity of Marvel Comics changed all that. Lee's new heroes allowed him to create something different from the typical "good-guy-versus-bad-guy" stories of old. From its very beginning, Marvel Comics focused more on the relationships between its characters and less on the typical conflict of heroes against villains.

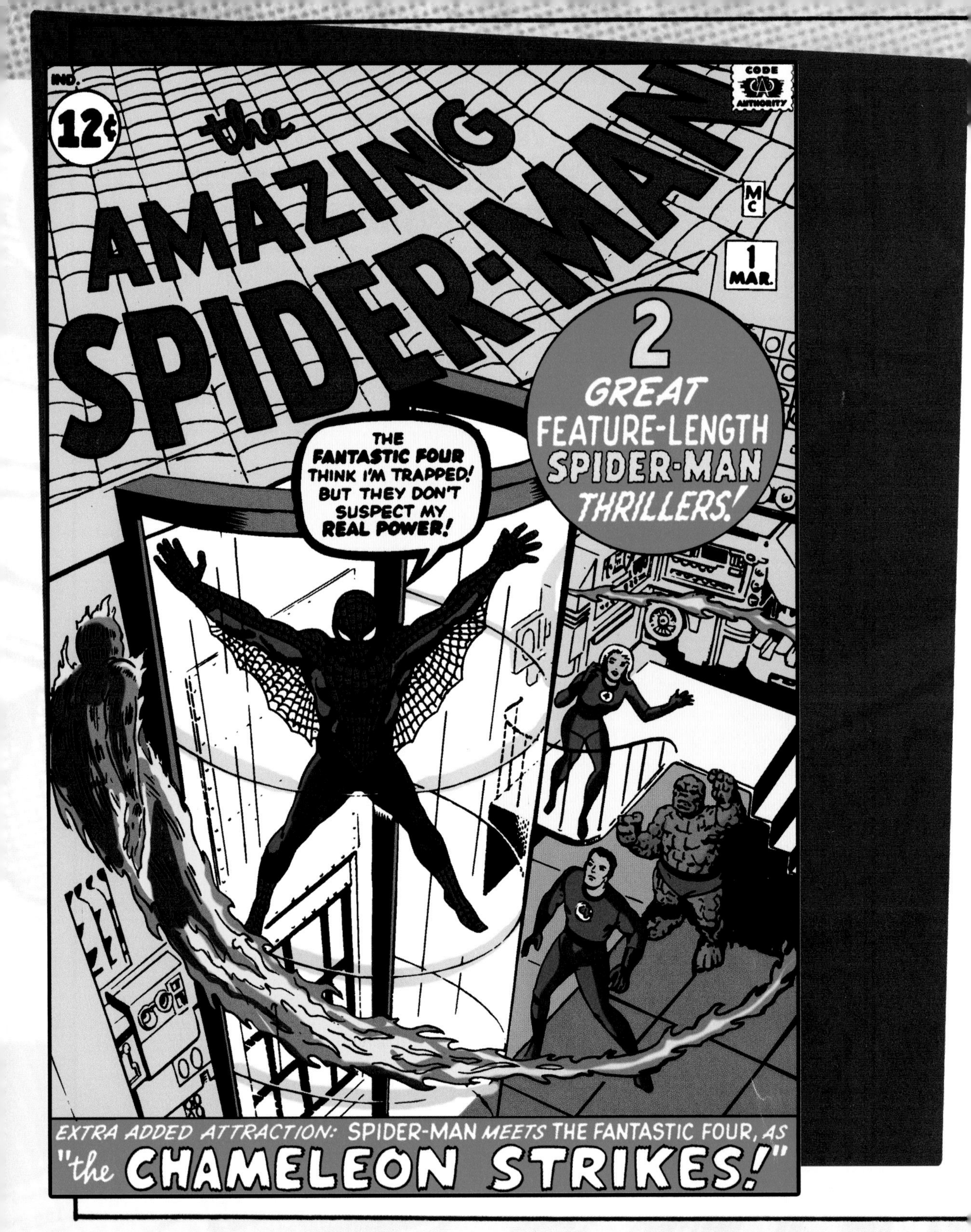
IND.
12¢
CODE AUTHORITY
the AMAZING SPIDER-MAN
MC
1 MAR.
2 GREAT FEATURE-LENGTH SPIDER-MAN THRILLERS!
THE FANTASTIC FOUR THINK I'M TRAPPED! BUT THEY DON'T SUSPECT MY REAL POWER!
EXTRA ADDED ATTRACTION: SPIDER-MAN MEETS THE FANTASTIC FOUR, AS
"the CHAMELEON STRIKES!"

Thanks to the contribution of Steve Ditko, Spider-Man evolved as an emotionally deep and rich character. In general, people could relate to Ditko's characters. They seemed to react with realistic emotions instead of the over-the-top melodrama that had been the standard for comic books up until then.

In *Stan Lee*, authors Jordan Raphael and Tom Spurgeon observed that by 1965, "Spider-Man offered an irresistible hook for outside observers . . . and a well-developed sense of emotional authenticity for those who were absorbed in his stories."

Equally important, the Lee and Ditko team had struck upon a formula that made it acceptable for readers to stick with comic books long past the age when they had previously put them aside. Marvel Comics suddenly made it cool to continue reading into high school and even college. The new formula also got older readers to start reading them again.

In an interview with Will Eisner, Jack Kirby said they did not recognize that Marvel had stumbled into new comic book territory until "some Columbia [University] students came up to Marvel, and . . . said the Hulk was the mascot of their dormitory. I realized we had a college audience."

**Within months, Stan Lee and Marvel Comics knew they had a hit on their hands with Spider-Man. The web-slinging Super Hero was given his own title in March 1963. Almost from the start, Lee had his Super Heroes existing in the same shared universe. For instance, he spiced up the first issue of Spider-Man's own title with a guest appearance by the popular Fantastic Four. (Cover shown at left.)**

# THE REAL LIFE

What readers seemed to like most about Spider-Man was Peter Parker. His life was familiar to readers because it mirrored their own. Most of them had experienced the same feelings of adolescent alienation.

## THE ORIGIN OF SPIDER-MAN

In Spider-Man's debut issue, the other kids in Peter Parker's high school class in Queens, New York, call our hero "Puny" Parker. He is frail and shy, a pampered orphan who lives with his elderly Aunt May and Uncle Ben.

Peter visits a science exhibit on experiments in radioactivity. While there, he is bitten by a spider that had accidentally absorbed "a fantastic amount of radioactivity." Feeling strange, the teenager steps outside. He is so focused on feeling his entire body "charged with some sort of fantastic energy" that he fails to see a car speeding toward him. Peter leaps out of the way, and that is how he discovers he now possesses incredible strength and can climb walls.

He realizes that the spider in some miraculous way has transferred its own power to him! Peter tests his newfound abilities for prize money in the wrestling ring. When he is successful, he decides to create a costumed alter ego for himself and go into show business to help support his family.

The masked Spider-Man is a hit. However, during his first public appearance, he fails to stop an escaping thief. This act will come back to haunt him, for the man he let escape turns out to be the burglar who later murders his beloved Uncle Ben.

"My fault—all my fault!" laments Peter. "If only I had stopped him when I could have! But I didn't—and now—Uncle Ben—is dead." As Peter walks off into the night, a caption tells us that he knows, at last, "that in this world, with great power there must also come—great responsibility!"

Being Spider-Man, however, made Peter's life even more complicated. Newspapers branded him a menace, and he found himself under constant attack from the likes of such villains as the Vulture, the Rhino, Sandman, Electro, Mysterio, and others. In addition, he also had to be careful with his frail old Aunt May. If she were to learn his true identity, the shock of the discovery might kill her!

Comic book readers had never seen characters with so much depth and real-life emotion. Prior to this, the standard comic story was short, and the plot was wrapped up quickly.

**Stan Lee and Steve Ditko were aware that their new character was not the typical Super Hero familiar to most comic readers. On the opening page of his introductory issue (above), they warned readers that Spider-Man would be "just a bit . . . different!"**

These new stories, however, were presented as continuing sagas, like TV soap operas. Their main stories and subplots continued from month to month, as well as from title to title.

Stan Lee and Steve Ditko—and the rest of the artists who co-created the Marvel stable of heroes—had revolutionized comics. Within a few years, the Super Hero would never be the same.

# MULTIMEDIA HERO

Spider-Man and his fellow Marvel heroes provided an invigorating blast of energy to the comic book industry. This exciting new approach rewrote the rules to the old concept of the costumed Super Hero. With their new way of doing things, Stan Lee and Steve Ditko caused a surge in sales not only at Marvel but at comic book companies across the board.

## THE SINCEREST FORM OF FLATTERY

Atlas Comics had once stayed in business by imitating others. Now, it had become Marvel Comics, the company that all the others wanted to imitate. Across the industry, comic book companies raced to grab hold of the successful Marvel

Comics coattails. Publishers who had abandoned their superheroes quickly revived them with new stories in an attempt to re-create the Stan Lee Marvel style. Of course, no matter how hard these competitors tried, they were missing the one vital ingredient to Marvel's success: Stan Lee.

The Marvel influence even began to seep into staid old DC Comics. By the end of the 1960s, young talents such as writers Dennis O'Neil and Mike Friedrich and artist Neal Adams were bringing real-life touches to DC's comics. These Ditko-type influences were most notable in the O'Neil-Adams collaboration on the groundbreaking *Green Lantern and Green Arrow*. Marvel had brought a more realistic approach to the characters themselves. Now, these new DC stories made it acceptable for Super Heroes to face real-life issues, from illegal drugs to racism to antiwar radicalism.

In 1971, Lee and artist Gil Kane took a courageous stand when they wrote a Spider-Man storyline that portrayed one of Peter Parker's friends as a drug abuser. This story defied the Comics Code Authority, which banned any mention of drugs in the comics it oversaw. However, the Comics Code could do little more than withhold its seal of approval for these issues. Lee's decision to defy the ban helped bring about changes to the rules. In the end, the Comics Code Authority changed its code, and comic book pages were allowed to show the negative effects of drugs. Ultimately, the incident moved comics forward, as publishers were allowed to tackle more adult subjects without fear of being banned.

Original artist Steve Ditko quit drawing *Spider-Man* in 1966. John Romita, an experienced romance and superhero artist, was called in to replace him. Romita's dramatic style was perfect for the scene, shown here, in which Peter Parker decides to quit being Spider-Man. It appeared in *Amazing Spider-Man* #50 (July 1967).

## SPIDEY AFTER STEVE DITKO

For reasons that he never made public, Steve Ditko left *Spider-Man* after drawing *Spider-Man* #38 (July 1966). In *Stan Lee*, Jordan Raphael and Tom Spurgeon write that behind the scenes, Lee and Ditko began to disagree on Spider-Man's direction. By issue #25, and perhaps several issues earlier, they explain, "Ditko was plotting the book himself and turning over the penciled pages to Lee, who filled in the dialogue . . . Then, one day in early 1966, Ditko walked into Marvel's offices on Madison Avenue, delivered a stack of pages, and quit." It is believed that Ditko resented the fact that Lee received the majority of the credit for the creation of Spider-Man. He may have also felt Lee did not appreciate the deeper emotional and philosophical issues that the artist was trying to bring to the stories.

# SPIDER-MAN IN OTHER MEDIA

Since 1967, Spider-Man has appeared on television, on the big screen, and in print media other than comic books:

- *Spider-Man* (ABC-TV)  Spidey's first animated series appeared on Saturday-morning TV from 1967 to 1970. It ran for fifty-two episodes.

- *The Electric Company* (PBS)  Between 1974 and 1976, a live-action Spider-Man popped in to teach vocabulary to the pre-school audience in eighteen episodes of this educational TV program.

- *Spider-Man* (CBS-TV)  After a successful 1977 TV movie, the web-slinger appeared in a live-action television show starring Nicholas Hammond as Spider-Man. The show lasted for only thirteen hour-long episodes.

- *Spider-Man: The Japanese Series* (Toei)  This live-action series ran for forty-one episodes on Japanese television, beginning in 1978. It featured a Spider-Man who was secretly Yamashiro Takuya, a motocross racer.

- *Spider-Man and His Amazing Friends* (NBC-TV)  This animated series costarred a number of other Marvel superheroes, including Firestar, and the X-Men's Iceman. It ran for twenty-four episodes, from 1981 to 1983.

- *Spider-Man: The Animated Series* (FOX)  This Marvel-produced series is considered by many the best and most faithful Spider-Man animated series. It ran for sixty-five episodes from 1994 to 1998.

*continued on following page*

Though sorry to lose his co-creator, Lee had to continue producing the monthly *Spider-Man*. So Lee turned to artist John Romita to replace Ditko. Romita began his career at Marvel in the 1950s, when the company was still called Atlas Comics, drawing such characters as Captain America. Romita had also drawn romance stories for DC Comics. While Romita's art was far less stylized than Ditko's, it was nonetheless firmly rooted in reality, a result of his many years working as a romance artist.

In spite of the loss of its co-creator, *Spider-Man* did not slow down. Stan Lee became a sort of comics cult figure, appearing regularly in the

*continued from previous page*

- *Spider-Man Unlimited* (FOX)  This animated series placed Spider-Man on an alternate Earth. It lasted only thirteen episodes during the 1999–2000 season.

- *Spider-Man* (Sony Pictures)  In this 2002 hit, Spidey was pitted against the Green Goblin. It starred Toby Maguire as Peter/Spider-Man and was directed by Sam Raimi.

- *Spider-Man* (MTV)  Featuring computer-generated graphics, this series ran for thirteen episodes in 2003.

- *Spider-Man 2* (Sony Pictures)  The 2004 blockbuster sequel, again starring Maguire and directed by Raimi, introduced Doctor Octopus to movie audiences. A third Spider-Man film is in production for 2007.

- Since 1978, Spider-Man has also been featured in some two dozen prose novels published by Pocket Books, Berkeley Books, Boulevard Books, Putnam, iBooks, and Del Rey.

> SPEAKING OF WHOM: SOME 1,500 MILES AWAY...

> THIS ISN'T DODGE CITY IN THE 1800's, HYDRO-MAN!

> SPLOOSH

Many artists left their mark on Spider-Man after Steve Ditko and John Romita. Canadian Todd McFarlane, for example, practically reinvented the web-slinger. McFarlane's wide-eyed, pretzel-limbed Spidey brought in many new fans and re-energized longtime readers, too. In this McFarlane illustration, Spidey takes on Hydro-Man in a panel from *The Amazing Spider-Man* #315.

media as the spokesman for the new generation of comic writers and artists. Marvel Comics remained the creative leader in the field throughout the 1960s, and Spider-Man remained the most visible example of the new wave.

## STAN LEE RETIRES FROM SPIDER-MAN

By the mid-1970s, Lee had given other writers the job of scripting *Spider-Man* and the rest of the Marvel titles. He later relocated to

California to develop Marvel's movie and television properties. By the late 1990s, Lee had taken the title chairman emeritus of Marvel.

The movie industry has long featured Super Heroes in high-budget films. Over the last few decades, however, Hollywood has shown increased interest in the genre. A big reason for the resurgence was the huge success of the movie *Spider-Man* in 2002. In the aftermath, an unprecedented number of comic book movies found their way to the screen. These included *Hulk*, *Daredevil*, *Elektra*, the *Blade* trilogy, and *The Fantastic Four* (all based on Marvel characters).

Spider-Man still appears in numerous ongoing comic book titles, including *The Amazing Spider-Man*, *Ultimate Spider-Man*, *Marvel Adventures Spider-Man*, and *The Sensational Spider-Man*. The web-slinger also appears in countless specials, spin-offs, miniseries, and one-shots. Of course, the character is also a continuing presence as an ongoing, syndicated daily newspaper strip (scripted by Stan Lee since its 1977 debut).

In 1990, Marvel launched a fourth monthly title starring the web-crawler, titled *Spider-Man*. Artist Todd McFarlane was the creative force behind the popular book. His style reminded older readers of Steve Ditko and struck a chord with the new generation of readers, too.

In spite of all the later developments, Spider-Man's true legacy remains his contribution to the evolution of the comic book. He will be remembered as the first Super Hero to emerge from the realm of disposable children's books to be accepted by adults as well.

# TIMELINE: STAN LEE AND STEVE DITKO

**1922**  Stanley Martin Lieber (Stan Lee) is born in New York City, December 28.

**1927**  Steve Ditko is born in Johnstown, Pennsylvania, November 2.

**1941**  Joe Simon and Jack Kirby leave Timely Comics; publisher Martin Goodman makes Stan Lee editor.

**1954**  Ditko begins working for Charlton Comics.

**1956**  Ditko does his first work for Atlas Comics.

**1961**  Atlas (formerly Timely Comics) publishes landmark *The Fantastic Four* #1, by Lee and Kirby.

**1962**  Lee and Ditko collaborate on *Amazing Fantasy* #7–14. Spider-Man, by Lee and Ditko, debuts in *Amazing Fantasy* #15 (August).

**1963**  Spider-Man appears in his own title, *The Amazing Spider-Man* #1 (March).

**1966**  Ditko draws *The Amazing Spider-Man* #38 (July), his last issue of the series.

**1968**  Ditko begins working for DC Comics.

**1979**  Ditko returns to Marvel to work on such titles as *Machine Man* and *Captain Universe*. He continues working for Charlton and DC.

**1980**  Lee moves to Los Angeles to represent Marvel properties in Hollywood.

**1996**  Lee signs a new contract with Marvel that names him chairman emeritus.

# SPIDER-MAN HIGHLIGHTS

**1962** Spider-Man, a character by Stan Lee and Steve Ditko, is introduced in *Amazing Fantasy* #15.

**1963** Publication of *The Amazing Spider-Man* #1, guest-starring the Fantastic Four.

**1966** Publication of *The Amazing Spider-Man* #38, the last issue of Spider-Man drawn by Steve Ditko.

**1971** Publication of *The Amazing Spider-Man* #96–98, in which Peter's friend Harry Osborn is revealed to be addicted to drugs.

**1973** Publication of *The Amazing Spider-Man* #118, Stan Lee's last issue as writer of Spider-Man.

In *The Amazing Spider-Man* #121, Gwen Stacy, Peter Parker's girlfriend, is murdered by the Green Goblin.

**1976** Publication of *Peter Parker, the Spectacular Spider-Man* #1, a new ongoing Spider-Man title.

**1977** *Spider-Man* syndicated strip begins running in newspapers nationwide.

**1984** In *The Amazing Spider-Man* #252, Spider-Man gets a new black costume.

**1985** Publication of *Web of Spider-Man* #1.

**1987** *Amazing Spider-Man Annual* #21 features the wedding of Peter Parker and longtime girlfriend Mary Jane Watson. The marriage is also featured in the June 5 installment of the Spider-Man daily newspaper strip.

**1990** *Spider-Man* #1, by Todd McFarlane, becomes one of the top-selling comic books up to that time.

**2000** Publication of *Ultimate Spider-Man* #1, a retooling of the Spider-Man story aimed at younger readers.

# GLOSSARY

**alienation** A feeling of unresponsiveness or hostility.

**enterprising** Energetic, independent, and willing to try new things.

**guru** One who is acknowledged as a leader with great wisdom.

**icon** An image or figure that stands as a symbol of something held in high regard.

**inker** The artist who goes over the penciler's lines with india ink in order to make the art reproducible.

**mandate** An order to be obeyed.

**melodrama** Events portrayed with exaggerated emotions.

**one-shot** In comic publishing, a storyline that is complete within one issue.

**panel** An individual frame, or box, on a comic book page.

**penciler** The artist who draws a comic book story in pencil; the work is later embellished by the inker.

**prototypical** Referring to a model on which something is patterned.

**syndicated** Term used to describe comics that the author sells to many newspapers or periodicals simultaneously.

Cartoon Art Museum
655 Mission Street
San Francisco, CA 94105
(415) 227-8666
Web site: http://www.cartoonart.org

Comic-Con International
P.O. Box 128458
San Diego, CA 92112-8458
(619) 491-2475
Web site: http://www.comic-con.org

Museum of Comic and Cartoon Art
594 Broadway, Suite 401
New York, NY 10012
(212) 254-3511
Web site: http://www.moccany.org

## WEB SITES

Due to the changing nature of Internet links, the Rosen Publishing Group, Inc., has developed an online list of Web sites related to the subject of this book. This site is updated regularly. Please use this link to access the list:
http://www.rosenlinks.com/crah/spid
You can also refer to Marvel's Web site:
http://www.marvel.com

# FOR FURTHER READING

Ditko, Steve. *Marvel Visionaries: Steve Ditko*. New York, NY: Marvel Comics, 2005.

Feiffer, Jules. *The Great Comic Book Heroes*. Seattle, WA: Fantagraphics Books, 2003.

Goulart, Ron. *The Encyclopedia of American Comics*. New York, NY: Facts on File, 1991.

Jones, Gerard, and Will Jacobs. *The Comic Book Heroes: The First History of Modern Comic Books from the Silver Age to the Present*. Roseville, CA: Prima Lifestyles, 1996.

Lee, Stan. *Marvel Visionaries: Stan Lee*. New York, NY: Marvel Comics, 2005.

Lee, Stan. *The Origins of Marvel Comics*. New York, NY: Fireside Books, 1974.

Lee, Stan, and Steve Ditko. *The Essential Spider-Man Volumes 1–7*. New York, NY: Marvel Comics, 2002.

# BIBLIOGRAPHY

Daniels, Les. *Marvel: Five Fabulous Decades of the World's Greatest Comics.* New York, NY: Harry N. Abrams, 1991.

Ditko, Steve. "An Insider's Part of Comics History: Jack Kirby's Spider-Man." *Robin Snyder's History of Comics*, Vol. 1, No. 5, May 1990.

Eisner, Will. *Will Eisner's Shop Talk.* Milwaukee, WI: Dark Horse Maverick, 2001.

Gross, Edward. *Spider-Man Confidential.* New York, NY: Hyperion, 2001.

Jones, Gerard. *Men of Tomorrow: Geeks, Gangsters and the Birth of the Comic Book.* New York, NY: Basic Books, 2004.

Lee, Stan. *Excelsior! The Amazing Life of Stan Lee.* New York, NY: Fireside Books, 2002.

Raphael, Jordan, and Tom Spurgeon. *Stan Lee: The Rise and Fall of the American Comic Book.* Chicago, IL: Chicago Review Press, 2003.

Simon, Joe. *The Comic Book Makers.* New York, NY: Crestwood, Il, 1990.

# INDEX

## A

Aunt May, 32, 33

## C

comic book/comics
  and college students, 8, 31
  criticism of, 17, 29
  history of, 5–6, 7, 8–9, 14–16, 17–18, 19,
    29–33, 34–35, 40
  and movies, 40
  readers' interest in, 6, 8, 16, 17, 29,
    31, 40
Comics Code Authority, 35

## D

Ditko, Steve, 7, 8, 18, 23, 27
  childhood of, 12–13
  departure from Marvel, 36, 38
  drawing style of, 13, 25, 28, 31, 34, 35,
    36, 38, 40
  influences of, 12–13

## E

Eisner, Will, 12, 31

## G

Goodman, Martin, 11, 16, 18, 20, 22–23

## H

Heck, Don, 18

## K

Kirby, Jack, 8, 11, 18, 23, 25, 27, 28

## L

Lee, Stan, 7, 8, 9, 10, 11, 12, 13, 22, 25, 28,
    38–39, 40

childhood of, 9–10
Fantastic Four and, 18–21
influences of, 10
after Marvel, 39–40
and military, 11
writing style of, 18, 21, 22, 26–27, 29,
    31, 34, 35

## M

Maneely, Joe, 18
Marvel Method, 26–27
McFarlane, Todd, 40

## P

Parker, Peter, 6, 22, 23, 32–33, 35
pulps, 14

## R

Robinson, Jerry, 13
Romita, John, 36, 38

## S

Simon, Joe, 11, 27
Spider-Man
  debut of, 5
  dispute over creation, 27
  impact of/success of, 5, 7, 28, 31, 32,
    37–38, 39, 40
  origin of, 32
  uniqueness of, 6–7, 22, 23, 25, 31, 33
  villains of, 33

## U

Uncle Ben, 32

## W

Wertham, Frederic, 17

## ABOUT THE AUTHOR

Paul Kupperberg is a writer and editor for DC Comics. He has published more than 700 comic books, stories, articles, and books, including two Spider-Man novels, *Crime Campaign* and *Murdermoon*. Two of his comic books, he is pleased to say, were drawn by the legendary Steve Ditko. The author has also published several years' worth of the *Superman* and *Tom & Jerry* newspaper comic strips. Kupperberg lives in Connecticut with his wife, Robin, and son, Max.

## PHOTO CREDITS

pp. 9, 15, 16 © Getty Images. All other images provided by Marvel Entertainment, Inc.

Designer: Thomas Forget
Editor: Christopher Roberts
Photo Researcher: Les Kanturek